INVITATION TO INTIMACY WITH GOD

Linda Rose Ingrisano

Copyright © 2024
Invitation to Intimacy With God

Cover Photograph copyright © 2024 by Aleacia Perdomo.
All rights reserved.

Locksmith Poem copyright © 2024 by Sally Kazin.
All rights reserved.

Diandra Garcia-Heredia, Editor
Frank Scott, Graphic Designer,
Digitalprismdesigns.com
Jay Wortham, Graphic Designer.

Linda Rose Ingrisano, Author,
Certified Spiritual Director/Companion
Franciscan University of Steubenville affiliate of The
Cenacle of Our Lady of Divine Providence School of
Spirituality. Spiritual Direction, January 28, 2006

St. Thomas University, Miami FL.
Spiritual Companionship, May 1, 2000
www.lindarose.net

Notice of Copyright
No part of this publication may be reproduced, stored, in a retrieval system or transmitted in any way by any means, electronic, mechanical, photocopy, recording or otherwise without the prior permission of the author except as provided by USA copyright law.

Printed in the United States of America
First Printing Edition, 2024.

Acknowledgements

I am so humbled and always amazed at how the Lord constantly sends such gifted, loving and faith-filled people into my life!
I received an absolute "yes" without hesitation when I asked each of these wonderful friends for their help with this project.

Contributors:
Reverend Dr. Eliseus Ezeuchene
Reverend Michael "Happy" Hoyer
Fr. Francis Pompei ofm
Drew Connor
C. Ann Getzinger, PHD, LMFT

Certified Spiritual Directors:
Debbie Grundel
Reverend Mister Randy Recker
Richard Filitor
Sally and Deacon Gerry Kazin

Thank you to all who have supported me by your prayers, patience, steadfastness, commitment, insights, love for Our Lord, but mostly for your friendship. I especially thank Frank Scott, Jay Wortham, Diandra Garcia-Heredia, Mary Wolski, and Fr. Ben Tomsen for their unending help in the completion of this project! As always I am thankful for all of my prayer partners…you will one day know the power of your prayers!

All Glory, Honor and Praise to the Father, Son and Holy Spirit both now and forever, Amen!!!

Note: Spiritual Directors are certified through the Franciscan University of Steubenville affiliate of The Cenacle of Our Lady of Divine Providence School of Spirituality, Spiritual Direction.

Letter From The Editor

Dear Reader:

I had the honor of working alongside Linda with her first 2 books: **Strength for Your Journey and Strength for Your Journey Devotional Companion**. Now I am thrilled to receive the "invitation" to once again work with her on **Invitation To Intimacy With God!**

Having the honor to work alongside Linda once more has been a new golden treasure of growth for me as I know it'll be for you. This time Linda revisits the Keys to the Kingdom of Heaven with a fresh twist, inviting us to add one more spiritual token to build those spiritual muscles-journaling.

I was reminded of my love for "writing it all down"; but really, I was reminded that the blessings that spring forth from it are indeed priceless, as Linda suggests. During a very new and challenging period in my life, I applied Linda's suggestions from these personal testimonies and spiritual leaders, psychology professional and compelling Scripture.

This project couldn't have come at a better time. My invitation to walk with the Lord in the most intimate way made all the difference in a month's time and well beyond!

She prayed with me. I prayed with her. We supported one another in health, love and friendship, meditation, and reflection.

We are blessed to have this text as a permanent tool for our current and future spiritual growth. As St. Ignatius says, "We experience and imagine ourselves in (that) scene" through Contemplation… Meditation (pondering) uses reasoning… both are used to come to know what God may be revealing to us. There is no right or wrong."

Now if that isn't enough to continue to keep the faith on your walk with Christ, just keep writing!

Your Editor with Love,

-*Diandra Garcia-Heredia*

About The Cover

While on vacation in Puerto Rico, my daughter, Aleacia, visited the Camuy Caves and took this photo. Discussing this book with her, I expressed a need for an inspirational picture for the cover. She excitedly said that she had the perfect one! When I looked at the photo, I was immediately inspired. Sometimes along our life's journey we encounter times of darkness, but faith tells us that God is always with us, giving us hope no matter what. He is the shining light in the darkness. Isn't it amazing that when she took the cover photo, the beautiful ray of light shined directly into the darkness? Thank you, Aleacia, for this stunning photo and for being an instrument of hope!

As I look back over my years of journaling, I become so aware of the fact that God, in His great mercy, has been with me every step of the way: guiding me, healing me, forgiving me, inspiring me, teaching me, holding me, and loving me. I then realize that I have truly entered an intimate, personal relationship with my God!

I pray that you, too, may experience this wonderful relationship with God, the One who loves you and created you as you practice this art of journaling!

Linda Rose

This Book is Dedicated to
Fishers of Men

Letter of Encouragement

Dear Reader,

We have heard that God is with us and we are seeking Him, and yet we don't fully know how. We find ourselves having heard something that invited us to find out more, yet we are somewhat blind to Christ's presence. Linda Rose Ingrisano, a great teacher and gifted author, in her newest bestselling book, shows you how to achieve that intimate, personal relationship with God. In just 30 days, Linda will instruct you by structuring your prayer time and guiding you on how to listen by pondering and journaling.

God has called you; He invites you to follow him and come to know Him and *Invitation To Intimacy With God* directs you to Him. No matter where you are today, God will bring you to a relationship with Himself.
This is no ordinary self-help book. This book is a one-of-a-kind challenge and is brilliant, life changing, transforming, and a soul-reflecting phenomenon.

You will be grateful to Linda Rose for her experiences that will help you listen and find the Lord. God is present with you, and you will know He is with you as you take up this challenge.

I highly recommend this book!
Don't wait another day to get started!
Do not miss this opportunity of gaining a personal intimate relationship and enjoy a great future with the Lord!
Thanks and praise the Lord,

-Reverend Michael "Happy" Hoyer
Chaplain Holy Cross Hospital at Ft. Lauderdale, FL

Table of Contents

Chapter 1	Introduction	Page 1
Chapter 2	The Key of Faith	Page 15
Chapter 3	The Key of Trust	Page 29
Chapter 4	The Key of Love	Page 39
Chapter 5	The Key of Obedience	Page 51
Epilogue		Page 65

Concordance:

Faith		Pages 77-80
Trust		Pages 83-85
Love		Pages 87-90
Obediance		Pages 93-95
Bibliography		Page 97

> To fall in love with God is the greatest romance; to seek Him the greatest adventure; to find Him the greatest human achievement.
> -*St. Augustine*

1
Introduction

It takes about 30 days to create a habit. I want to challenge you to practice the habit of listening to God by pondering and journaling for one month. By this, you will enjoy that intimate, personal relationship with God. I know you can do it! I hope that you, as a reader, will take me up on this month's challenge…

The blessings that will come to you are priceless, so please don't give up. In this book, I will share some Keys to Freedom[1] and tools to help structure your prayer time and guide you on how to listen. Trust me, this works. This is like joining a boot camp: if you want to build your muscles, you join a boot camp.

This is like joining a Boot Camp for the Kingdom of Heaven[2] ! If you want to have a relationship with your Creator whom, by the way, knows you, made you and has a plan for your life, join this Boot Camp for the Kingdom of Heaven.

"For I know well the plans I have for you," declares the Lord, *"plans to prosper you and not harm you, plans to give you hope and a future. Then you will call on me and come and pray to me, and I will listen to you. You will seek me and find me when you seek me with all your heart. I will be found by you,"* declares the Lord. **Jeremiah 29:11-14**

Not too bad, right?

Embarking on this month's challenge will lead you to that intimate relationship with God, and you will be transformed!

Dear Reader,

Journaling has given me not only the ability to see what lies just below the surface of my experiences, but more importantly, what's at the core of them.

Since I am currently in the CPE (Clinical Pastoral Education) at a hospital, it's hard not to think of a medical analogy for journaling. When working in the trauma center, I see many patients come in with wounds and conditions of various sorts. From gunshot wounds, broken bones, and heart attacks they all come into the emergency room seeking help.

While some are caused by accidents, many are the result of injury caused by another, and still others are self-inflicted. In each of these scenarios, much information can be gained by visual inspection, asking questions, and assessing the level of pain. But in each case, an Xray or MRI is required to find out either what damage has been done, or what is causing the condition or pain, thus leading the care team to the appropriate treatment for the patient.

My experience with journaling has been much the same. I know what happened in a particular event in my life and how I feel or felt emotionally, but until I stop, pray, and explore what is below those base level functions, I may never know the "why" of the matter.

This is by no means reserved for those things in our lives that can result in pain and suffering, quite the contrary. By engaging in this process, I can develop a keener sense of what's going on in the depths of my soul, where God is working, and what He wants me to see and learn from the experience.

In journaling, I have found a voice that I never knew I had. I can distinguish and more importantly, for me, articulate all that's going on inside of me. It gives clarity in understanding my mental, physical, emotional state not otherwise visible at first glance. There is something very raw and organic about it that reveals the true self, unfiltered and pure. It is a gift given to us by God to interpret the "movings" of the Holy Spirit in our lives and an opportunity to receive the grace to act on those prompts that lead us closer and closer to the Holy Trinity with certainty and boldness.

I firmly believe this process of going deeper in contemplation has brought me to where I am today as a transitional Deacon headed into the Priesthood. There have been so many miraculous events in my life that could have and would have gone unnoticed unless I was intentional about searching for them.

Often when I review what was written in my journal, I wonder who wrote it. These are the very things that I cannot normally articulate, describe or define, but they come across with such lucidity that I know it is the Holy Spirit working in and through me.

-Reverend Mister, Randy Recker

A Little About Me

I felt like I was in the wilderness. My life…my dreams…all fell apart. I had no job. I was alone. I felt so abandoned and rejected. I felt worthless and afraid. All seemed dark and hopeless. I didn't know how to go on. I had faith in God, but that didn't seem to help me…I searched for years. I heard so many testimonies from wonderful, faith filled people about how God guided, healed, and helped them on their own life's journey. They seemed to grow into peaceful people who were strong and "had it together" despite their trials. They seemed to know God personally, and they believed Him so they were able to walk in Trust!

However, as for me I still didn't get it. I thought I was following God, but when it came to my life's struggles, I was lost. I didn't know how to use what I believed to attain healing, help, and most of all peace. I wanted joy! I wanted to be one of those people who knew how to handle life's curves without it destroying me.

I will make a roadway in the wilderness. **Isaiah 43:19**

This is the Scripture I heard deep within my heart during one of the most difficult times in my life. For the next seven years as I learned to listen to God, I received many tools and revelations that I entered in my journal, which helped me understand how to trust God and stand on my faith. I gradually learned how to grow into a spiritually free soul who had the ability to act on my faith rather than react from my dysfunction. I came into a deep personal relationship with my Father in Heaven. He continues to guide, heal, strengthen, teach and comfort me.

We are all called to *"Go into the world. Go everywhere and announce God's goodness to one and all."* **Mark 16:15-20**

All of us are called to "spread the Good News" to "fish" for others to bring close to Christ! To become Fishers of Men, you will need to have a personal relationship with God. How will you be able to bring others to Christ if you don't know Him?

Did you ever wonder how your faith in God would help you when your life's journey brings trauma, loss, sickness, and disappointments with so many trials? If you are truly seeking answers about your life's journey, you will need to have that personal, intimate relationship with your Father in Heaven.

Having this relationship takes time…time to talk…time to listen…time to share your life, including your hopes, dreams, joys, hurts, etc. In your spiritual life, this is called prayer.

Prayer is the essence of your spiritual life and takes time to adjust to. As God leads you, you will begin to enjoy a personal encounter with Him. As you read on, look at this as a practice manual for the exercise of prayer.

Most people who know me know that I love the TV series, Star Trek. I just love watching as they explore strange new worlds and seek out new civilizations! They had no guidebook on the ways of that new world, and this resulted in many hardships, trials, tribulations, etc. Sound familiar?

Unlike the Star Trek team, we do have a guidebook the Bible to show us how to live in the Kingdom of Heaven. Jesus tells us that we are in this world but not of this world. When we follow God, we are living in an alien world. I love this, don't you? The Kingdom of Heaven; His ways, His laws are so opposite of humanity. Think about it: Pray for your enemies; do good to those who hate you; thank and praise God in all circumstances… that means all the time plus give 10% of your work earnings back to God.

Now, how do we do this? How do we act the opposite of what we have learned all our lives? We grew up in this world, shaped by our families of origin, teachers, cultures, experiences, traumas, disappointments, etc.

Much of what we have learned on our unique journeys is good; however, our actions are often a result of what we have learned in the world, and they may prohibit us from ACTING on God's ways. How do we become spiritually free to act on our faith rather than react from our brokenness?

Enter the Boot Camp for the Kingdom of Heaven…practice prayer using the tools of the Four Keys to Spiritual Freedom: Faith, Trust, Obedience and Love. Practice reading, meditating, listening, and journaling… and learn how to use the many principles found here in this guidebook.

Dear Reader,

Journaling to me is an important step in understanding my spirit and journey. God's Spirit feeds me a little at a time. This is His way. He lights my path one step at a time so as not to overwhelm me. When I reflect back to my journal, I discover the Spirit's enlightenment.

Reflecting back to each day, week, month or year shows me how much He is in control and I see His love and my growth in understanding it. Journaling also reveals to me my purpose and brings new, different or deeper meaning to my life's journey. Without journaling my life would be a random path and I would not be able to connect His holy dots of love.

However, it is not always easy to accomplish. Regular prayer time is essential but is just one piece of the holy process. There are, at times, life issues that get in the way as well as dryness, desolation and countless other distractions. The evil one has many tricks and tactics and uses each moment, especially when we are journaling and listening for God's way.

Additionally, I have learned that I need a goal, or type of spiritual structured learning process (by myself or in a group) i.e. a book on spirituality. To me the most enjoyable and surprising result of journaling after meditating and/or contemplating and thanking God on a particular reading is that after I start to write God takes over. I think that I have a pretty good idea of what I have received and what I will write but then God takes over!

Words, thoughts, situations, people, past events etc. that did not come to me are suddenly being written by me. All this guides, heals and teaches me, it is God's Love and Grace!

This is the most astonishing part of journaling: God speaking to and through me by my pen and paper. This is the spiritual food I crave. God is good all the time. All the time God is good.

Spiritual Director, Richard Filitor

God speaks in the silence of the heart, and we listen. And then we speak to God from the fullness of our heart, and God listens. And this listening and this speaking is what prayer is meant to be. **Mother Teresa**

Prayer is the place of refuge for every worry, a foundation for cheerfulness, a source of constant happiness, a protection against sadness. **St John of Chrysostom**

A servant of the Lord is he who in body stands before men, but in mind knocks at heaven with prayer. **St John Climacus**

Prayer preserves temperance, suppresses anger, restrains pride and envy, drawsdown the Holy Spirit into the soul and raises man to heaven. **St Ephraim the Syrian**

And while it has not pleased the Almighty to bless us with a return of peace, we can but press on, guided by the best light He gives, trusting that in His own good time, and wise way, all will yet be well. **President Abraham Lincoln (Annual message to Congress on December 1, 1862)**

When a Christian shuns fellowship with other Christians, the devil smiles. When he stops studying the Bible, the devil laughs. When he stops praying, the devil shouts for joy. **Corrie Ten Boom**

Don't worry about having the right words; worry more about having the right heart. It's not eloquence he seeks, just honesty. **Max Lucado**

Pray, and let God worry. **Martin Luther**

Prayer is the easiest and hardest of all things; the simplest and the sublimest; the weakest and the most powerful; its results lie outside the range of human possibilities they are limited only by the omnipotence of God. **Edward McKendree Bounds**

Some important notes:

Please don't read ahead. Take one chapter at a time.

Do the prayer assignment each day of the week. Contemplate or meditate. Ponder what you read, and then record it in your journal.

Contemplation, according to St. Ignatius, uses imagination. We read a Scripture verse, or a memory comes to mind. We experience and imagine ourselves in that scene.

Meditation (pondering) uses reasoning. We think about the meaning of the words we just read. Both are used to come to know what God may be revealing to us. There is no right or wrong. Whichever you decide is ok, just do it! For the sake of ease, I will use the word "ponder" when referring to contemplation or meditation.

This is a month's walk with the Lord: Be patient… persevere… ponder… take your time.

If Catholic, try to attend Mass and Adoration of The Blessed Sacrament as much as possible during this journey.

At Mass and while meditating in front of The Blessed Sacrament, I enter the mystical Holy Presence of my Lord and Savior and am reminded of **Psalm 46:10:** *Be Still and Know that I am God.* It is during these times, while looking up and not around, I am guided, healed, forgiven, inspired, taught, and loved!

The journey is just that, a journey, your journey. God will bring you where He wants you in His time. There will be many bumps, distractions, and interruptions along this road. But that's ok…keep going!

If you are attending the Fishers of Men breakfast, you will be given a journal unless you already have one. While listening to the speaker and witness talk, record anything that comes up for you it could be a word or something that the presenter said that struck you. You may have time after the talk to elaborate about what you heard.

Later at home, take the time to settle in a quiet place and look over what you have written…ask the Holy Spirit to speak to your heart… read it again, ponder, and record in your journal. Don't worry if you get interrupted or you aren't receiving anything. Let go and go about your day letting what you read resonate; then come back later when you have quiet time.

Use this form of journaling while attending a retreat, Christian conference, or Bible study. It is in your reading, pondering, and journaling where the Lord will speak to your heart.

Here are a few suggestions to get in the habit of "pondering":

- Allocate time each day for prayer. Invite the Holy Spirit to speak to your heart. Read the text and read the question for the day. Connect with God through heartfelt conversation, expressing your gratitude, concerns, and desires.
- Practice either contemplation or meditation to allow for Divine guidance and inspiration to flow into your life.
- Maintain your journal by documenting your experiences during this challenge.
- Prayerfully look back over your journal each week.
- This process will help you reflect on your spiritual growth, recognize patterns, and gain clarity on how God's love and guidance are manifesting in your life!

Tip: If after prayerfully looking over the week's journaling, you see that you have not received anything after pondering, pray:

Thank you, Holy Spirit, for showing me the root reason why I have not received anything.

Say this prayer as you continue your ponderings in your prayer time until you receive the answer.

Don't worry! This is the reason journaling is so important: the fact that you didn't receive anything, tells you something. Trust the Lord. He will enlighten you.

Now let's try...

Read the Introduction and record in the spaces below what came up for you after reading the question of the day. Do the same for each day this week.

QUESTIONS TO PONDER ON THE INTRODUCTION

DAY 1: What is your prayer life like? Can you recall a time when God answered your prayer? Record in detail.

_____

_____

_____

_____

DAY 2: Are you seeking God's will? In what ways do you feel yourself seeking God's will?

_____

_____

_____

_____

DAY 3: How do you feel about the Bible being your guidebook?

_____

_____

_____

_____

DAY 4: What do you think Jesus meant when he said, "We are in this world, not of it"? What are some ways you have experienced God's ways being different from those of man?

_____
_____
_____

DAY 5: As you read the introduction, what ideas came up for you?

_____
_____
_____
_____

DAY 6: Pick a quote from the box on page 7. Meditate, ponder, and journal on that quote. Record insights/revelations that you received.

_____
_____
_____
_____

DAY 7: Prayerfully look back over your journaling. Record anything that stands out.

_____
_____
_____

> Acquire the habit of speaking to God as if you were alone with Him, familiarity and with confidence and love, as to the dearest and most loving of friends.
> *-St. Alphonsus Ligouri*

Notes

2
A Key for Spiritual Freedom

THE KEY OF FAITH[3]

Because I am an artistic type of person, I relate to color and images, so...let's color the Key of faith green. Just as our green earth is our foundation for physical buildings: Faith is the foundation for the building of our spiritual life.

Remember that we are not of this world, we are in this world. We are challenged to act on our faith, not react from our dysfunction! My faith is what I have built my life upon. It is my hope, dream, and purpose. It is my healing; my comfort; my stability; my end and beginning! Without my rock of faithful living, what would be left? What is my purpose? Why am I alive? I believe that I have been fearfully and wonderfully made **Psalm 139:14** that God began a good work in me, and He will perfect it until Jesus comes **Philippians 1:6**...that I am gifted for the purpose of glorifying God, that God is with me always and knows me better than I know myself. So I can put all my faith in Him!

When do you first remember learning about your faith? Was there someone who inspired you? Perhaps you grew up in an abusive situation or were the victim of trauma, loss, or any number of other tragedies, unable to wrap your head around the concept of faith, much less God if He is real, where was He for me? Hopelessness creeps in when we believe in an unloving God who seemed absent during challenging times.

I had a real problem with that very thing: If God is real, where was He for me? Where was He when I lost all my material possessions; my child suffered; my marriage fell apart, and my dad died in a tragic boating accident?

How do I have faith in someone who I can't see or hear, who is supposed to love and care for me? It took lots of repeated decision making to try believing to try to stand on faith. I had to look at the walls I built within myself, the false visions I had of God because of my life experience with men and various other challenges. Remember this: We are not "of this world, we are in it!"

We are to act on what we believe... this our faith alone, not on our own vision, reasoning, imagination, or our brokenness. (Hint: Acting on Faith brings Trust!)

If you find that you just can't understand many things in your life or worry and have anxiety, anger, disappointment, fear, and you are unable to act on your faith: ask for faith and thank God for giving you faith!!! God will give you more than you can imagine. God will give you the Grace to look up and not around!

Despite our false visions of God, life experiences, trials, traumas, disappointments, and failures, we need to decide repeatedly to have faith in Him, His Word, and His ways even when things make no sense and when circumstances become overwhelmingly painful.

Because my dysfunctional actions and thoughts have brought so much pain, failure, and grief into my life, I turned to the Word of God for guidance. I decided to believe. The Lord gave me the grace to have faith in His Word and His ways.

I especially love the Psalms! In them I find a roadmap for living in the Kingdom! In the Psalms, I find healing words, strength, guidance, and proper ways to act and think everything I need to walk in the ways of GOD.

In contemplating **Psalm 23**, for example, during a time of rejection, abandonment, betrayal, shame, and loss, the Lord gave me these revelations:

The Lord is my Shepherd, I shall not want.

It is His job to supply all my needs food, shelter, emotional support...

He makes me lie down in green pastures. He restores my soul; He guides me in the paths of righteousness for His name's sake.

He will take all my burdens, hurts, and brokenness to bring healing. He will guide me on the way that is aligned with His will.

Even though I walk through the valley of death, I fear no evil, for You are with me, Your rod and Your staff, they comfort me.

When I am in the pit and I don't see any way out, I must know that You are with me and that You will be my strength.

You prepare a table before me in the presence of my enemies; You have anointed my head with oil, my cup overflows.

You set the time, space, and circumstances in front of my enemies. You anoint me with your Holy Spirit and pour down Your overflowing graces so that I can love You.

Surely goodness and loving kindness will follow me all the days of my life!

When I obey and do what God wants me to do, goodness and kindness will be with me always and in all ways.

And I will dwell in the house of the Lord forever.

When I walk with the Lord in his Kingdom, I am eternal.

I would like to share an experience I had that demonstrates acting on Faith:

I lead a musical ensemble: *Linda Rose & Company*. We, along with a ministry named *Answered Prayers Project*, were once invited to lead worship and minister to women at *The Mary Hall Freedom House* in Atlanta, Georgia. There are four backup singers in the ensemble and three musicians. The singers and I bought airline tickets, and the three musicians planned on driving up. Well, about a week before the trip the musicians informed me that they were not able to go. Each had a good reason, but *what now?* How will we sing without any instrumentation?

Normally I would have cancelled the "gig", but four of our singers bought tickets and took days off of work to be there! In the past I would have felt guilt.... fear... embarrassment... anxiety... I would have been so stressed out... crying... thinking of what a disaster this was. *Why did I think I could do this? Who did I think I was?* Instead I prayed with Faith: I went to the Lord and affirmed: *Well, Lord, apparently You have someone else in mind that You want to have play with us. Thank You for guiding me to find that person!*

The next morning when I woke up, I had the idea to call a friend of mine in Atlanta who I had sung with in the past. When I asked her if she or another friend would be available, she informed me that it would be impossible for them, but she gave me the name of someone who might help. I called this young man, told him my story, and asked if he would be available. He said, *Sure, I am off on Mondays and would love to play for you!* Furthermore, I asked what he does for a living - to which he replied, *I am the music minister for the Catholic Liturgies at Emory College and work part-time at St. Peter Channel Church here in Atlanta.* Wow! God is so good he was also gracious enough to bring with him a bass player!

I didn't even mention that I couldn't even get in touch with the Founders of the Mary Hall Freedom House to finalize timing and the program schedule: Could we get into the room so that the sound equipment could be delivered, and we could practice? After all, we had not played with these musicians and didn't even know if they knew the music! *Answered Prayers Project* was also coming to set up... on and on. Needless to say, this was an experience in acting on Faith.

The blessings were incredible! Since I went to the Lord with this challenge, **I was gifted with peace and confidence that God had my back!** I even laughed at the seemingly messed up plans! The keyboard and bass players seemed like they had played with us forever! It turned out that one of my sons played drums with us and another son sang with us! Double the blessings. The backup singers were so "in tune," and the women that attended were amazing. They stood, sang, and worshiped with us. What a glorious opportunity to spread the Good News. This was so much more than I had ever expected or dreamed of. What a glorious opportunity to spread the Good News. This was so much more than I had ever expected or dreamed of.

When we act on our Faith… *Look up instead of around…* there is no telling what God will do!

Dear Reader,

Faith has always been a big part of my life. I would like to say the same about journaling… but no. I began journaling at the request of my first spiritual director about 25 years ago. Journaling has not always been easy for me; however, I have found it important to my spiritual growth and my relationship with my Lord.

One example of how journaling helped in my spiritual growth is as follows: I was reviewing my journals about one incident. I began to recognize patterns of behaviors and challenges that have been a part of my life, which had yet to be overcome. In my writings, I saw the same behavior over and over.

I took this to God in prayer. I was then given the grace to see my repeated behaviors and reactions, then the Lord reminded me to "love my enemies." It was like a lightbulb went off and I was able to see MY part in this circumstance. I knew that MY attitude had to change.

I couldn't keep sticking my head in the sand expecting OTHERS to change. As I continued to ponder this situation, I felt God was asking me to forgive them and myself as well. I knew that it is not my job to fix anyone. After all, He is the Savior!

I began to realize that I had to keep my eyes focused on Jesus, not on myself and my feelings. I saw my lack of humility, my lack of patience, rash judgment, etc…

I realized then that God would give me the graces I would need to grow into a more loving servant for Him. I would be able to hold my tongue and my thoughts to myself.

I still struggle, but I thank God for speaking to my heart, for helping me to grow in virtue, so that I can pass his love onto others. Through God's grace I can keep a deeper faith and trust in him.

Journaling helps me recognize what a loving, wonderful God I serve, and I am blessed to bring everything to him in prayer.

Spiritual Director, Debbie Grundel

Your faith may be just a little thread. It may be small and weak, but act on that faith. It does not matter how big your faith is, but rather, where your faith is.
Rev. Billy Graham

To one who has faith, no explanation is necessary. To one without faith, no explanation is possible.
St. Thomas Aquinas

If you believe what you like in the gospels, and reject what you don't like, it is not the gospel you believe, but yourself.
Saint Augustine

We are twice armed if we fight with faith. There is but one cause of human failure. And that is man's lack of faith in his true self.
Plato

Faith is not the belief that God will do what you want. It is the belief that God will do what is right.
Max Lacato

There are two primary forces in this world, fear and faith. Fear can move you to destructiveness or sickness or failure. Only in rare instances will it motivate you to accomplishment. But faith is a greater force. Faith can drive itself into your consciousness and set you free from fear forever.
Norman Vincent Peale

Additional Prayer:

AN EVENING PRAYER FOR HEALING:

Please begin to pray the following prayer each evening for the rest of the month.

Holy Spirit, I give you permission to enter into my subconscious mind and bring me healing while I sleep.

In the same way, the Spirit helps us in our weakness. *We do not know what we ought to pray, but the Spirit himself intercedes for us through wordless groans.* **Romans 8:26**

I love this! The Holy Spirit knows where I need healing and growth. Sometimes He brings it to my attention, so I can use the tools shared here to work on what comes up, and other times He just does the healing while I am asleep without me even knowing!

This prayer has been such a great blessing to me over the years. I have learned that the Lord will never push Himself on me, He is a gentleman. Therefore, we need to invite Him in.

Now as you go through this challenge, I know that the Lord will bring to your mind areas where you need growth.

Remember, He made you and knows all about you. He desires to heal, guide, and teach you so that you may become the person he created you to be!

Together with the reading, pondering, journaling, and saying this prayer each night, the Holy Spirit will heal, guide, teach and love you! You will become aware of the personal, intimate relationship that our Lord desires of you.

Dear Reader,

After more than 25 years as a Licensed Marriage and Family Therapist, I firmly believe that personal journaling is one of the best and quickest means to make progress in spiritual growth for both myself and my clients.

This process awakens both your conscious and unconscious mind. Your mind may be occupied with your daily struggles, but you may be unaware of many underlying issues in your unconscious mind.

I begin my journaling with a prayer to the Holy Spirit and a question that is my issue for that day. Next, I pray with praise and thanksgiving for my blessings before I ask for insight about my concerns.

Since the Holy Spirit knows me completely, my mind will be open to thoughts, feelings, and older memories that may "float" to the surface. I recommend handwriting, since your mind works faster than your hand and leaves room for the Holy Spirit. I always receive an answer; an inspiration, scripture, a hymn verse, or perhaps from a sermon or spiritual reading.

Whatever I receive, it is a gift from the Holy Spirit. Many of my clients have tried journaling with their own therapeutic issues. Many receive helpful inspiration, or issues which they explore in therapy. Though journaling may seem difficult, it is well worth the effort since it is such a fruitful practice.

C. Ann Getzinger, PhD, LMFT

QUESTIONS TO PONDER ON FAITH

Pray the evening prayer.

Holy Spirit, I give you permission to enter into my subconscious mind and bring me healing while I sleep.

DAY 1: What is Faith to you? When did you first realize you had Faith? Was there a person in your past that helped you with Faith?

_____
_____
_____

DAY 2: Read and meditate on **Psalm 139**. Do you have faith that God loves you and has gifted you for a purpose?

_____
_____
_____

DAY 3: What obstacles in your life prevent you from having more faith: learned behavior, past traumas, disappointments?

_____
_____
_____

DAY 4: As you read this chapter on Faith, what came up for you? Explain in detail.

DAY 5: Go to the **Concordance** on pages 77-80. Pick a Scripture passage on Faith, ponder and record in your journal.

DAY 6: Pick a quote from the box on page 21. Meditate, ponder, and journal on that quote. Record insights/revelations that you received.

DAY 7: Prayerfully look back over your journaling. Record anything that stands out.

___

As the Holy Spirit brings areas that need healing or growth, look to the **Concordance** for extra Scriptures on **Faith**, pages 77-80. Ponder and record.

> Faith is, above all, a personal, intimate encounter with Jesus, and to experience his closeness, his friendship, his love; only in this way does one learn to know him evermore, and to love and follow him evermore. May this happen to each one of us.
> *-Pope Benedict XVI*

3
A Key for Spiritual Freedom

THE KEY OF TRUST[4]

Crystal... the perfect diamond is truly crystal clear, harder than steel and flawless. One who trusts the Lord sees through his or her daily trials as if they were transparent. Through those trials, they see the Lord's abiding love transcend. They see that trust in Him is perfect, flawless, and not easily broken.

Trust, in my experience, takes time... 30 long years, in my case! When I came to the Lord 30 years ago, I delved into Scripture. I was so hungry for God's Word! At that time, I was walking through one of the hardest trials of my life: I gave birth to a son who had multiple heart defects, and I was told that he would die before he was five months old. In my sorrow and struggle, I turned to God for some sense to all of it. As I read Scripture little by little, believed His Words to be true and acted on them, trust grew in my heart. I used my Faith key and made the decision again and again to believe in God's ways...not mine!

As I decided to trust God's words, He blessed me with endurance, wisdom, hope, peace, and that blessed assurance that He was with me, understood me, cared for me, would heal me and be with me no matter what happened to my son. I even got to the point, within my heart, where I knew that God loved my son more than I ever could. And if He decided to take him home (heaven), I knew it was for my son's ultimate good! I attained peace with it! Now that's trust!

As I read through Scripture, I came across **Psalm 143:5**, which says........*Meditate on My doings.*

As the years went on, I accumulated a long journal of "God's Doings" in my life. I wrote what was happening in my life; that is, my joys, sorrows, hurts, and praises.

Scripture reading became a part of my life as I found answers in God's word hope, support, healing, joy, grace, council, guidance, and so much more! I recorded all of it in my journals. They became journals of "God's Doings" (God's words in action) in my life, and this has been a great gift to me! These doings are very valuable because when I doubt, when I look around and not up, when I act on my dysfunction, I have my journal to look back on and "meditate on God's doings" to help me remember what God has done for me. It is then that I realize **my God can be trusted!**

Maybe you are like me, and you have been deeply wounded by life's many trials without placing trust in God. Maybe you have placed your trust in money, your job, your spouse, your traditions, your dreams, and any number of other things.

You might do this simply because it is what you have been taught, or maybe it is a defense mechanism. Whatever the reason, if you aren't placing your trust in God…His Word… Christ…you will continue having a false sense of security.

DO NOT PLACE YOUR TRUST IN:

Weapons Psalm 44:6

Wealth Psalm 49:6-7

Leaders Psalm 146:3

Man Jeremiah 17:5

Works Jeremiah 48:7

Man's righteousness Ezekiel 33:13-15

Instead… PLACE YOUR TRUST IN:

GOD'S NAME Psalm 33:2

GOD'S WORD Psalm 119:42

CHRIST Matthew 12:17-21

In those times of desolation, those times when I couldn't feel God, believe He was there or believe I was loved, somehow, I had the grace to reach out to God. Each time He answered me. It was His grace, His unmerited, abundant, and merciful love for me! I used my Trust Key. I immersed myself in the Scriptures God's words to me and I began taking God at His Word. Over time I got to know my God personally and intimately and I realized that He is totally trustworthy! Totally faithful!

Another Scripture that caught my attention is Jesus saying: *Truly I say to you, unless you turn and become like children, you will never enter the Kingdom of Heaven.* **Matthew 18:3-4**

Wow, this made me think about children…what was so special about them regarding trust? Think of the innocence of a little child. They don't worry about what they will eat or wear. They don't worry about how they will have money to buy all the necessities; in fact, they don't worry because they TRUST! They trust that their caregiver will meet all their needs without even realizing it. They don't rely on their own reasoning, dreams, imaginations, or experiences. They live in total trust. This, my fellow followers of Christ, is exactly what we are commanded to do.

You cannot see what God is doing in your life. You cannot see the Lord's abiding love for you during your trials if you don't trust Him as a child! When you look around at the circumstances at the world and use your reasoning, your imaginations, your judgments, you are simply not trusting God.

You are leaning on your own understanding.

How can you figure Him out? God sees all of eternity! God knows you inside and out because He made you! He loves you! He sees your beginning and end and everything in between! He already knows what you need! He is your loving Father…your Caretaker…who can be trusted! He desires a personal, intimate relationship with you to help you become more like Him and grow in holiness, spending all of eternity with Him!

A PERSONAL LETTER TO YOU

My Child,

You may not know Me, but I know everything about you. **Psalm 139:1** *I know when you sit down and when you rise up.* **Psalm 139:2** *I am familiar with all your ways* **Psalm 139:3** *even the very hairs on your head are numbered.* **Matthew 10:29-31** *For you were made in My image.* **Genesis 1:27** *In Me you live and move and have your being* **Acts 17:28** *for you are my offspring.* **Acts 17:28** *I knew you even before you were conceived.* **Jeremiah 1:4-5** *I chose you when I planned creation.* **Ephesians 1:11-12** *You were not a mistake, for all your days are written in My book.* **Psalm 139:15-16**

I determined the exact time of your birth and where you would live. **Acts 17:26** *You were fearfully and wonderfully made.* **Psalm 139:14** *I knit you together in your mother's womb.* **Psalm 139:13** *And I brought you forth on the day you were born.* **Psalm 71:6** *I have been misrepresented by those who don't know Me.* **John 8:41-44** *I am not distant and angry but am the complete expression of love* **1 John 4:16** *and it is My desire to lavish My love on you* **1 John 3:1** *simply because you are My child and I am your Father.* **1 John 3:1** *I offer you more than your earthly father ever could* **Matthew 7:11** *for I am the perfect Father.* **Matthew 5:48** *Every good gift that you receive comes from My hand* **James 1:17** *for I am your provider and I meet all your needs.* **Matthew 6:31-33** *My plan for your future has always been filled with hope* **Jeremiah 29:11** *because I love you with an everlasting love.* **Jeremiah 31:3**

My thoughts toward you are countless as the sand on the seashore. **Psalm 139:17-18** *And I rejoice over you with singing.* **Zephaniah 3:17** *I will never stop doing good to you* **Jeremiah 32:40** *for you are My treasured possession.* **Exodus 19:5** *I desire to establish you with all My heart and all My soul.* **Jeremiah 32:41** *And I want to show you great and marvelous things.* **Jeremiah 33:3** *If you seek Me with all your heart, you will find Me.* **Deuteronomy 4:29** *Delight in Me and I will give you the desires of your heart* **Psalm 37:4** *for it is I who gave you those desires.* **Philippians 2:13** *I* *am able to do more for you than you can possibly imagine* **Ephesians 3:20** *for I am your greatest encourager.* **2 Thessalonians 2:16-17** *I am also the Father who comforts you in all your troubles.* **2 Corinthians 1:3-4** *When you are brokenhearted, I am close to you.* **Psalm 34:18** *As a shepherd carries a lamb; I have carried you close to My heart.* **Isaiah 40:11** *One day I will wipe away every tear from your eyes* **Revelation 21:3-4** *and I will take away all the pain you have suffered on this earth.* **Revelation 21:3-4** *I am your Father and I love you even as I love My son, Jesus* **John 17:23** *for in Jesus, My love for you is revealed.* **John 17:26** *He is the exact representation of My being.* **Hebrews 1:3** *He came to demonstrate that I am for you, not against you* **Romans 8:31** *and to tell you that I am not counting your sins.* **2 Corinthians 5:18-19** *Jesus died so that you and I could be reconciled.* **2 Corinthians 5:18-19** *His death was the ultimate expression of My love for you.* **1 John 4:10**

I gave up everything I loved that I might gain your love. **Romans 8:31-32** *If you receive the gift of My son Jesus, you receive Me* **1 John 2:23** *and nothing will ever separate you from My love again.* **Romans 8:38-39**

Come home and I will throw the biggest party heaven has ever seen. **Luke 15:7** *I have always been Father and will always be Father.* **Ephesians 3:14-15** *My question is…will you be My child?* **John 1:12-13** *I am waiting for you.* **Luke 15:11-32**

With love,

Your Dad, Almighty God[5]

QUESTIONS TO PONDER ON TRUST

Pray the evening prayer.

Holy Spirit, I give you permission to enter into my subconscious mind and bring me healing while I sleep.

DAY 1: What do you place your trust in? Explain in detail.

_____
_____
_____
_____

DAY 2: Recall a time when you decided to trust God…what was the outcome?

_____
_____
_____
_____

DAY 3: Who in your life is trustworthy? Why?

_____
_____
_____
_____

DAY 4: Have you ever placed your trust in someone and been disappointed? Explain. Have you ever thanked anyone for being trustworthy? What was the outcome?

___

DAY 5: Read and meditate on the Scriptures on Page 30. What are the benefits of putting your trust in God? Give examples in your own life.

___

DAY 6: Read and meditate on the Father's Love Letter. What comes up for you? Explain.

___

DAY 7: Prayerfully look back over your journaling. Record anything that stands out.

___

As the Holy Spirit brings areas that need healing or growth, look to the **Concordance** for extra Scriptures on **Trust**, pages 83-85. Ponder and record.

> God communicates the mystery of the Trinity to this sinner in such a way that if His Majesty did not strengthen my weakness by a special help, it would be impossible for me to live.
> *-St. John of the Cross*

Notes

4
A Key for Spiritual Freedom

THE KEY OF LOVE[6]

The Key of Love is red. The heart is the center of the body bringing forth life giving nutrients to all the other parts of the body. Without it, the body cannot function. So also, love is the heart of our spiritual body The BODY of CHRIST. Love calls us to forget ourselves and to give freely, using all the gifts that we have been given. Thus, the body of Christ becomes a life-giving organism throughout the world.

When I first did a study on Love in the Scriptures, I was very surprised to learn that love is not a feeling. It is a verb, an action!

We know love by this that He laid down His life for us; and we ought to lay down our lives for the brethren. But whoever has the world's goods and sees his brother in need and closes his heart against him, how does the love of God abide in him? Little children let us not love with word or with tongue but in deed and truth. **1 John 3:16-18**

Also, in another Scripture we see another great action verb......and what an action God did for us! God gave his son for us!

For God so loved the world, that he gave his only begotten son. **John 3:16**

Jesus is the greatest example of love. Let's look at history as it unfolded in the Bible.

God instituted animal sacrifice through the shedding of blood for the atonement of sins. He killed an animal to make clothes to cover Adam and Eve when they sinned against Him. In the book of Leviticus we learn that God gave extensive instructions on how, when, and under what circumstances animal sacrifices were to be offered to Him in atonement.

This is the Law that God gave to Moses. This Law was to continue until Christ came to offer the ultimate perfect sacrifice which made animal sacrifice no longer necessary. These animal sacrifices were only temporary. Humans continued to sin; therefore, sacrifices were done continuously in accordance with the Law.

Jesus died for our sins. Jesus wasn't merely human. If He was, then His sacrifice would have also been a temporary one because one human life could not possibly cover all the multitudes of human sin, nor could one finite human life atone for sin against an infinite God.

The only viable sacrifice must be an infinite one, which means only God Himself could atone for the sins of mankind. Only God Himself, an infinite being, could pay the penalty owed to Him. Therefore, God had to become a Man and dwell among men **John 1:14**. No other sacrifice would suffice. Jesus, as God incarnate, sacrificed Himself. He laid down His life willingly.

Greater love has no one than this: to lay down one's life for one's friends. **John 15:13**

Jesus became the blood sacrifice in atonement for our sins, and Jesus' once-for-all-time sacrifice was followed by His resurrection. He laid down His life and took it up again, thereby providing eternal life for all who would ever believe in Him and accept His sacrifice for their sins. He did this out of love for the Father and for all those the Father has given Him. Can you imagine such an act of love?

Over the years I have witnessed many acts of love given by many of my brothers and sisters in the Lord. As I previously shared with you, I lived for many years with my son who had the heart defects. Many times, the hospitals would be in another state, which required plane fare to say the least. I was part of a wonderful church community. Sometimes I would get a moment's notice to fly my son to the hospital out of state. That same day I would be greeted with plane tickets and money to go… we sometimes would be gone for months, but upon my return my kitchen would be stocked with food!

In another incident, I witnessed another act of love: I received a call from someone whose daughter was running from an abusive husband. She left with her baby. Someone came forward and found an empty apartment for her but then she needed furniture. I told her not to worry that God would not leave her alone. I praised and thanked God for getting her what she needed. (I used my Faith and Trust Keys!)

The next day the Lord led me to someone who knew someone else who worked in a facility which held some extra furniture and household items. They were willing to give it to her for free. The amazing thing is that within a day people came forward to help with the picking up and delivery of the furniture! When we arrived at the facility, another miracle took place. It turned out that two of the people in charge of giving away the furniture were once in that same situation. And by the time we left, we were given the entire contents of a full two bedroom apartment! Sheets, blankets, towels, dishes, pots, lamps…everything one could ever need. We were all thanking and praising God for all the gifts, for the open hearts of all who came to her aid, and mostly for the Love, the action taken for this woman and her baby!

Engage in acts of kindness and compassion towards others like this, whether it's offering help, listening attentively, or simply being present for someone in need. These acts can open your heart and allow God's Love to flow through you!!!

Dear Reader,

I was asked to give a witness talk at a Fishers of Men breakfast, and as I sat down to prepare my notes, the first thing I did was pull out my journals. I did this to remind myself of the many things I learned during our various gatherings during the past 4 years.

Why journal? Studies have shown that within 10 minutes after a presentation we remember only 50% of what was said. Within 24 hours that number then drops to 25%. By the end of the week, it is somewhere around 10%. Yet if you take notes, you are likely to retain 100% of what was said, if not retain, you can always refer to your notes as I have done.

Have you ever realized that when you journal, you are acting like the disciples John and Matthew? If they had not written down what they had seen our Lord do and say, where would we be today?

As I looked over my journals, I was prompted to look back over my life. I then became aware of the many moments that I was guided (inadvertently) by the Holy Spirit.

The following are some of those moments:

I had been given the nerve (grace) to ask a beautiful woman for a date that flourished into a life of marriage that has lasted 39 years. My first visit to the Catholic Church. Though this was not the first time I had been in a church, it was the first time I felt an overwhelming warmth or presence making me feel welcomed and at home.

I remember hearing a priest say, "We must be present with the Lord." That reminded me one of the hardest times in my life: Our eldest son was born October 16, 1986. After years of trying, we were finally pregnant. It was the happiest day but also the scariest, for he had the umbilical cord wrapped around his neck and had a bowel movement. Only 10% of babies at that time survived during this type of delivery. Doctors rushed in as his heart rate dropped, had me sign paperwork and escorted me out of the room as we were both afraid that we would lose our first born.

I went into this white hallway, leaned against the wall and prayed asking the Lord to please spare this little baby. I asked to forgive me for my mistakes so far in my life, and I promised to turn my life around.

A year later as we prepared to have our son baptized, the Lord held me to my earlier promise in a phone call from the nearby Catholic pastor. He said, "Mr. Connor, I see by your paperwork that you attend Mass once a month." To which I said, "Yes, father."

He went on. "Well as a good practicing Catholic, you should be attending Mass at least once a week and confession once a month." To which I replied: "But I am not a Catholic." After a long pause the father says, "Are you interested?" "Why, yes", I replied, and the following Easter I was Baptized, Confirmed, and received my first Holy Communion.

I was later asked (led) to become an Extraordinary Minister of the Eucharist, which I have continued to serve to this day 34 years later. As I became aware of the Lord's presence, I was led to take Holy Communion to the sick at a nearby hospital.

The floor I was led to volunteer was an AIDS and Oncology Ward. Bringing Holy Communion was such a blessing for me to be able to share with these people the body of Christ and to share Scripture. There were times when people were near death, and I was able to help and comfort the family. I realized it was the Holy Spirit working through me to help bring His lost sheep home.

In the summer of 2013, I was diagnosed with Non-Hodgkin's Lymphoma and would undergo chemotherapy every 3 weeks for 4 months. As a result of the chemo, I would have a very compromised immune system, so I could no longer go to Mass or take communion to the sick in the hospital.

I hated not being able to attend Mass and missed serving the Lord as I was accustomed to. As the Lord brought these happenings to my memory, I became so overwhelmed with tears because of the wonderful love and support I received from many in the church during this most difficult time. I also became aware of how the Lord allowed me to comfort, serve and love others.

P.S. I have been healed of the cancer!

Seven years later, I helped to start a ministry called Justice & Peace using material purchased from JustFaith. Little did I know that it was also developed as a tool for The St. Vincent de Paul Society of the United States. To this day I volunteer with St Vincent De Paul Society. This is and has been the best thing I could have done. That feeling I first felt when I went to Mass with my wife was the same feeling I had when calling on our "neighbors in need." We are called to take care of the poor, regardless of their religious affiliation or circumstances.

Each time we an help someone, it is the same feeling one feels as a child on Christmas morning. We have been able to help others, while serving as witnesses of our Lord and Savior.

It is often when no one else is around and I am meditating, praying, or sleeping that I will have a bright new idea. Little do I realize it is not my idea, but it is the Lord, the Holy Spirit, nudging me, coaching me, guiding me to love and serve those around me. I am then inclined to record all of this in my journal to remind myself of all the many blessings that the Lord has showered upon me.

During my time with cancer and to this day I have not been afraid, for I have come to that deep personal relationship with my Lord. I trust and know that He is with me. He has blessed me with an angel of a wife, two loving sons who married two beautiful supportive women. He has given me opportunities to serve and love others...

What a treat to reflect upon these memories in my journal. How awesome is Our God!!!

-Lay Minister, Drew Connor

Love is the only force capable of transforming an enemy into friend.
Martin Luther King, Jr.

And remember, as it was written, to love another person is to see the face of God.
Les Misérables

Love never claims, it ever gives.
Mohandas K. Gandhi

Love is that condition in which the happiness of another person is essential to your own.
Robert A. Heinlein

Not all of us can do great things. But we can do small things with great love.
Mother Teresa

The Christian does not think God will love us because we are good, but that God will make us good because He loves us.
C. S. Lewis

QUESTIONS TO PONDER ON LOVE

Pray the evening prayer.

Holy Spirit, I give you permission to enter into my subconscious mind and bring me healing while I sleep.

DAY 1: What does it mean to you that Jesus became the blood sacrifice for your sins?

_____

_____

_____

_____

DAY 2: What has Jesus overcome? Do you live as an overcomer? If so…How? If not… why?

_____

_____

_____

_____

DAY 3: Record a time when you witnessed Love as action…Explain in detail.

_____

_____

_____

_____

DAY 4: Record a time when you missed an opportunity to love…How did you feel?

DAY 5: Go to the **Concordance** on pages 87-90. Pick a Scripture verse on Love. Ponder and record in your journal.

DAY 6: Pick a quote from the box on page 45. Meditate, ponder, and journal on that quote. Record insights/revelations received.

As the Holy Spirit brings up areas that need healing or growth, look to the **Concordance** for extra Scriptures on **Love**, pages 87-90. Ponder and record.

Remember: He wants your fellowship, and he has done everything possible to make it a reality. He has forgiven your sins, at the cost of His own dear Son. He has given you His Word, and the priceless privilege of prayer and worship.
-Billy Graham

Notes

5
A Key for Spiritual Freedom

THE KEY OF OBEDIENCE[7]

Deep blue is the color of the ocean. Without water, all life withers and dies. Likewise, without obedience, our spiritual life withers and dies. We must be ready to submit our will to the Lord and say, your will be done if we wish to feed our spiritual life and keep it alive. Obedience is, oddly enough, a key to freedom.

Obedience is submission to authority. In our case, it is submission to God. I have found this very difficult to follow. I was used to doing my own thing! I never really thought about the fact that I was following my own desires, dreams, and imaginations. I just went on with my life and kept running into trouble! When I finally found the Lord, rather when He finally got my attention, I began to read the Scriptures and realized that I needed to follow God's ways and not mine! I had to be submissive to Him…to OBEY His Word…to keep His commands!

Keeping the Lord's commandments means to hold, to keep or observe God's commands firmly to obey. This, my brothers and sisters, is the work. This is Spiritual Exercise! This is what I call the Boot Camp for the Kingdom of Heaven! Remember: if you want to become physically fit, commitment to an exercise routine is a must. If you want to live in spiritual freedom and follow God's will, a commitment to spiritual exercise is a must.

Setting a regular time aside for prayer; reading God's word, asking the Holy Spirit to enlighten you; listening with your heart to "hear" what God is saying and practicing obedience.

This takes time and effort, but the results are awesome for your soul! If you will take the time and commit to these exercises, you will be able to walk the walk, not just talk it. And don't forget: Act on God's ways, and don't react from yours. Then you will be spiritually free!

I had a profound experience the first time I ever obeyed God's word… My son was four years old and getting ready for his fourth experimental open heart procedure. The doctors informed me that he had a 15% chance of survival. As you can imagine, I was beside myself and could not imagine myself taking my son by the hand to lead him to what could be his death.

The night before, in my sorrow and torment, I went to the Scriptures and came upon **1 Thessalonians 5:18**:

In ALL things give thanks; for this is God's will for you in Christ Jesus.

The word ALL stood out. Give thanks in ALL things! I found it hard to believe that God would ask me to thank Him for everything in my present situation. In my desperation, I decided to try it. I began thanking God that I had food and a place to live. Then I thanked Him for the hospital, doctors and their abilities and training. I was thankful for my son's life, of course. I got closer and closer to the idea of thanking God for this situation. And I finally said the words, Thank You, Father, for what is happening in my son's life!

I fell asleep with those words on my lips, exhausted from hours of crying and agonizing searching the Scriptures. When I awoke the next morning, I had Peace! I was filled with Grace! It was as if I'd not just gone through all that turmoil the night before. I had a peace that I could not explain… I was able to be strong for my son to speak peacefully with him and calm him. And I was able to stay with him as he fell asleep for the surgery. It was such a blessing for us.

In the years following and in my reading of the Word, I found many commands that we are told to obey.

Let all bitterness and wrath and anger and clamor and slander be put away from you, along with all malice. Be kind to one another, tenderhearted, forgiving one another, as God in Christ forgave you. **Ephesians 4:31-32**

Wow, there is much to say about these commands, but I will focus on forgiveness. I don't know about you, but for me this is impossible to do without the help of God.

Over the years I have prayed with many people who have gone through many devastating circumstances and traumatic events. They have had the opportunity to obey God and forgive those who have been their abusers. Those who decide to act on God's Word and not react from their "stuff" experienced much healing emotionally, spiritually and physically! They walked in spiritual freedom. Those who continue in their stubborn resentment stay in their heartache, torment, and any number of other physical illnesses.

Forgiveness. This is so hard, yet it is commanded of those dedicating their lives to following Jesus. This is the work (the spiritual exercises, the Boot Camp for the Kingdom) we are required to obey! Why is it so hard? Is it because of our judgment? After all, we say, they were so wrong in what they did or said…everyone agrees! Is it because of our pride? Does it have to do with our shame, fears, past traumas?

The issue of resentment usually has a root in us. And we are so unaware of it. We can't forgive because of our own dysfunction; our own will gets in the way. We do not know what we are doing! The results are devastating to others and to us! We hurt and destroy ourselves and each other by our hatefulness, and then we blame them!

Practice forgiveness towards yourself and others. Reflect on any grudges, hurts or resentments that you may be holding onto. And make a conscious decision to release them to God. Embracing forgiveness will bring healing. Open your heart to experience God's love more fully.

Do not misunderstand me.

Yes, sometimes we are innocent victims of someone else's "issues", but I am talking to you about forgiveness…your response to God's command.

As for the person who has wronged you how do you come to terms with what they have done or said that has hurt you so deeply and caused devastation in your life and sometimes in the lives of others? If you are using your own judgment… your own set of rules…your own vision and imagination… it will be very difficult to forgive!

Go back to your Faith and Trust Keys and remember that we walk in the Kingdom of God, it is like an alien world. God's ways are not our ways, and forgiveness takes time. Just because you say the words I forgive so-and-so does not mean that you will feel it! Just be obedient and God will do the rest! You will know that the forgiveness…healing… is complete when you can see the person or circumstance as a **gift** in your life!

Dear Reader,

The task of journaling documenting a divine prayer experience or encounter often seems to be one that is either readily embraced by some or firmly rejected by others. Often journaling is mistakenly seen as a burdensome, daily, homework assignment for which there is little personal benefit, or maybe the objection to journaling is unclear, which in itself could have meaning.

Whatever personal perspective one may have, journaling is objectively a spiritual tool by which the faithful collect and assemble puzzle pieces of discovery so the true image of God and self may emerge. In an artistic sense, journaling is a means to understand how the Potter is fashioning our lives or how His brushstrokes on the canvas of our soul are becoming a masterpiece.

In a practical sense, keeping a prayer journal is a way we map the steps we've taken in the spiritual journey to better understand from where the Lord has taken us and to where He is leading us. Regardless of the degree by which we may embrace the habit of journaling, journaling is a necessary practice with the purpose of spiritual growth. I recall the first time a spiritual director asked me to journal.

Initially the thought of keeping a journal of my most private thoughts seemed childish, risky, laborious, and a waste of my time, so at first I resisted and relied on memory to describe my prayer experience to him.

He patiently encouraged me to keep a prayer journal, so out of obedience, I eventually did. I soon realized my written notes helped me to remember simple but important details that would otherwise slip from my fallible human memory, a loss Moses cautioned the Israelites about near the end of their historic desert journey from Egypt (Dt. 4:9). So, despite my unwillingness (or laziness!), I persisted to jot down notes after my prayer time so I could later share them and make monthly spiritual sessions more revealing of God's formative work in me.

A prayer journal became a means to prepare for spiritual direction rather than being a useless historical record of my life. By recalling specific instances in which I encountered the Lord both within and beyond formal prayer, I grew to better understand my true self and the true image of Him like collecting breadcrumbs of revelation along the spiritual journey toward holiness.

I learned first-hand why the word "journal" is intrinsically linked to the middle English word for "a period of travel" ("journey") and "importance" (e.g., a "journal" bearing).

Years later journaling is still a habit for me. I've become aware which of my conversations with the Lord are "journal worthy" (e.g., about two or three entries each week that I ought to remember to discuss next with my director). By recording my key encounters with the Lord, spiritual themes, revelations, and obstacles emerge more readily for discussion than they would have from my dimming memory alone. After my director and I discuss them, I draw a line after the last entry in my journal so I can focus on subsequent entries for future sessions.

I rarely go back into old journals unless the Spirit (or my director) ask me to, but none the less, I could with great clarity if I had to, which is why a spiritual journal grows in value with time. If a deeply important revelation from God seems vague or altogether lost with age, my prayer journal becomes a map by which I can rejoice to find lost treasure!

With respect for the elements of a journal entry (made almost always after prayer since meditation and disposition are opposing skills!), there are usually five: 1) the date 2) the scripture prayed (prayer with the Word must always include his word!) 3) the principle spiritual affection by which the Spirit led me into dialogue with Him (Ignatian!); 4) a brief summary (usually one, grammatically incorrect sentence or even sketch) of my prayer experience or revelation; and 5) a plea for God's help His grace related to the substance of my prayer or personal need.

Whether we embrace or resist journaling, there is the benefit of spiritual growth in it for everyone. It is a necessary tool that helps to clarify our prayerful meditations, ones "… Christians owe themselves lest they come to resemble the first three kinds of soil in [Jesus'] parable of the sower." (CCC 2707) We journal what the Lord writes on our heart as He dialogues with us in prayer, just as He wrote His commands on two stone tablets following the Great Theophany. If the Maker of heaven and earth bothers to write down what he's likewise spoken, perhaps we should also!

Spiritual Director, Deacon Gerry Kazin

In all His acts God orders all things, whether good or evil, for the good of those who know Him and seek Him and who strive to bring their own freedom under obedience to His divine purpose. All that is done by the will of God in secret is done for His glory and for the good of those whom He has chosen to share in His glory.
Thomas Merton, No Man Is an Island

Forgiveness is an act of the will, and the will can function regardless of the temperature of the heart.
Corrie Ten Boom

To be a Christian means to forgive the inexcusable, because God has forgiven the inexcusable in you.
C.S. Lewis

Obedience is not measured by our ability to obey laws and principles; obedience is measured by our response to God's voice.
Dwight L. Moody

Faith is only real when there is obedience, never without it, and faith only becomes faith in the act of obedience.
Dietrich Bonhoeffer

QUESTIONS TO PONDER ON OBEDIENCE

Pray the evening prayer.

Holy Spirit, I give you permission to enter into my subconscious mind and bring me healing while I sleep.

DAY 1: Practice cultivating an attitude of gratitude by regularly expressing appreciation for the blessings in your life. Make a list of things you're grateful for and record them in your journal. Then take a moment to thank God for his love and provision.

_____
_____
_____
_____

DAY 2: How do you feel about submitting your will to God's will? Have you ever obeyed His will over yours? What was the outcome?

_____
_____
_____
_____

DAY 3: Read Psalm 19:7-14 and complete these verses and record what comes up for you:

a. The law of the Lord is perfect…

b. The testimony of the Lord is sure…

c. The precepts…

d. The command…

e. The fear…

f. The judgment…

DAY 4: What does the concept of "Boot Camp" as it relates to our spiritual exercises mean for you? Explain.

_____
_____
_____
_____

DAY 5: Have you ever experienced forgiving someone or yourself? How did you do it and what was the result? How did you feel?

_____
_____
_____
_____

DAY 6: What might hold you back from offering forgiveness? Could it be pride, shame, fear, or past traumas?

_____
_____
_____
_____

DAY 7: Prayerfully look back over your journaling. Record anything that stands out.

_____
_____
_____
_____

As the Holy Spirit brings areas that need healing or growth look to the **Concordance** for extra Scriptures on Obedience, pages 93-95. Ponder and record.

> If we do not fill our mind with prayer, it will fill itself with anxieties, worries, temptations, resentments, and unwelcome memories.
> *-Scott Hahn*

Notes

EPILOGUE

As you approach the end of the month challenge, take time to reflect on your journey. Look back over your journal. Celebrate the growth, insights and experiences God has graced you with!

Consider using these tools and practices beyond the challenge.

Remember this is a personal and individual experience with your relationship with God. Stay open, receptive, and committed to your spiritual journey and trust that God's love and guidance will accompany you along the way!

Lastly, become part of a supportive Christian Community, this can provide encouragement, inspiration, and a powerful sense of belonging.

MORE TO PONDER

Hopefully you have experienced the Lord speaking to your heart after taking up this challenge! I pray that you will continue to use this invaluable "tool" along your journey!

One of my dear friends, Fr. Pompei OFM, gave me permission to print the following excerpt from his book: **The Most Important Book You Will Ever Read.**

The question here is "Does the Lord really communicate and talk to you?" Rather than me trying to explain the answer to you, I have included the various ways that others and myself have a dialogue relationship with Jesus below.

THROUGH A SITUATION:
A young man named Tim, senior in college, decided to take an alternative Spring Break and volunteered for a week at St. Francis Inn Soup Kitchen in Philadelphia. His plan was to get his master's degree in engineering, but after living and working with the poor, feeding them, waiting on and befriending them, He experienced the Holy Spirit and Jesus. In his own words, "I actually felt Jesus in the people when I spent time talking and serving them." Does the Lord communicate and reveal His Will to us? You bet He does. How do I know that? Tim postponed his grad school plans and volunteered two more years at the soup kitchen.

THROUGH THE WORD OF GOD:
When my sister faced cancer and surgery, she was overcome by fear and worry. She initially asked the Lord for a miracle. When her fear intensified and she became more anxious, she opened her Bible and read words of Jesus that jumped off the page, as if Jesus was right there saying them to her personally.

"While you are in the world you will suffer, but don't be afraid, for I am with you. Trust in God and Trust in me."

She prayed for healing but prayed for the grace to Trust in Jesus and let go of her fear by not dwelling on her cancer and surgery. Instead she focused on the Lord with her and on doing things she would ordinarily do to keep her attention from centering on her cancer. It was not magic, because that's not how Trust works.

She was still tempted and attacked by fear, but kept choosing to tell Jesus she trusted Him, and she let go. Little by little, the grace she asked for was given to her, because she experienced peace and less and less fear and worry.

The day of her surgery, two of her friends and I were waiting for the doctors to call her down. We prayed with her and again she simply said, "I trust in you, Jesus. Your Will be done." When we finished, my sister who has a great wit, made us laugh with funny one-liners about her surgery. All of us, my sister included, felt absolutely no fear or worry.

When the doctor and nurse walked in, we were having a full belly laugh. Later the doctor told my sister that in all his years doing surgery, he never experienced someone so unafraid and overcome with laughter as they wheeled her into surgery. My sister told him that Jesus told her to trust Him, and she did. Does Jesus communicate and reveal his will for us through His words? You bet He does. Just ask my sister.

DIRECT FROM THE LORD:
My brother, now a retired diocesan priest, while on a long retreat as a young priest received two direct words from the Lord, calling him to a prophetic preaching ministry. He made the leap of faith and trusted in the Lord, and his life and ministry changed radically.

Since that time he has preached and given the Lord's Word and prophecies to many thousands of people all over the United States and Europe. He has also prophesied to the institutional church, parishes, and individuals. Like many prophets, he was mocked, belittled, and considered a 'persona non grata' (someone unwanted or appreciated in a setting). However, by trusting in the Lord and living by the guidance of the Holy Spirit, Jesus has been able to forgive, heal, guide, and give hope to many more people than he would have if my brother stayed in parish ministry.

Does Jesus reveal His Will and Plan for our lives directly? Ask my brother!

"For to one is given by the Spirit the Word of Wisdom, to another the Word of Knowledge by the same Spirit." **1 Cor. 12:8**

CHURCH TEACHINGS:
All Christian religions believe in the forgiveness of our sins, because of Jesus shedding His blood on the cross with the saving words, "Father, forgive them for they know not what they do."

Phil is a man I visited in a maximum-security prison who had attempted suicide a couple times for his horrific crimes, feeling nothing left to live for.
He was an atheist his whole life and lived according to his own desires and beliefs. I told him there was another way besides suicide, and that I knew how to lead him there, without preaching to him or trying to proselytize him.

In short, I told him that the God who created Him would not only forgive him, but He unconditionally loved Him before he sinned, while he was sinning, and after he sinned.

I left him with a decision to make. If you hate your life, would you be willing to give it to Jesus and ask for His forgiveness? He said Yes the following week, and we prayed together. When he was praying and surrendering his life to Jesus, he burst into hysterical sobbing, and all of his self- hatred poured out. Then he looked up at me, half-dazed and said, "Jesus is really here, isn't He?" I said, "I guess so, and He really loves you." The Christian church teaches that Jesus forgives our sins. Ask Phil if he not only believes this but experienced it. Phil is no longer an atheist.

THROUGH OTHERS: (Sometimes the most unlikely)
Yes, the Lord can and does answer our prayers through other people, and sometimes by those we least expect. They can even be unaware that they are the answer to your prayer. The Lord can bring more good out of this way of answering your prayers, because you just may be the answer to theirs. The Lord doesn't force us, but sets up the connection of people and hopes we are open to giving to one another not only answers but also Peace of Mind, healing, and even forgiveness. Let me explain.

PERSONAL STORY:
When I was at a soup kitchen in Philadelphia where we fed 300 people a day, twice a day, we friars lived across the street from the kitchen in a row house in what the TV program Nightline reported was one of worst neighborhoods in the United States.

There were always five to ten people sleeping on cardboard on the sidewalk in front of our door and at the soup kitchen. I couldn't sleep one night, decided to go outside to the kitchen to get some milk.

For two or three weeks, I was going through the motions, but inside I was "burnt out," getting conned, threatened, and constantly ripped off.

I started becoming cynical and questioned what I was doing with my life. I sure did not feel like a Franciscan priest or 'brother' to the people.

When I walked out of the friary onto a piece of cardboard, there he was, "Cincinnati", as he wanted to be called. He was one of the worst con men at the kitchen, and I was his worst confronter. We were like oil and water.

So he immediately woke up as I opened the door, got up on his knees and told me he had to go to the bathroom and that he was hungry. I wasn't in the mood for his lies and con job, so my first response was No. Then he kept demanding and begging as usual. So, reluctantly, he followed me to the soup kitchen. I opened the door of the bathroom and waited for him to finish. As he left, he saw two donuts left over from the day before and asked to take them, once again in his demanding voice. I simply said Take them. All I wanted to do was get a glass of milk.

When I finished and started walking back to the friary, I remember thinking "Not a great start of the day again, Lord. I have no idea where you are and what's happening to me."

When I got to the friary door, there was Cincinnati waiting for me. What did he want now? Then he put his hand on my shoulder, looked at me with a look that I had never seen before, touched my cheek, and with a heartfelt voice said, "Brother Francis, you are a real Brother."

After three weeks of self-pity, the Lord spoke and reminded me who and what I was, that He had been with me and loved me. That's the adventure of the Lord. His answer to my prayer came through a poor homeless person named Cincinnati.

After that morning, we became friends, but he still conned me. However, it was a lot less. And when he did, we'd both laugh. So keep your spiritual eyes and ears open for the answers to your prayers, because Jesus is full of surprises. You can end up with more than you ask for.

CONNECTING DOTS: GUARANTEED 'ADVENTURE'
Did you ever meet someone, a complete stranger, and circumstances led you to help them? Or, they helped you in a way that really answered both of your prayers? Afterwards, as you reflected on it, you felt that it was not a coincidence, rather it had been planned by the Lord without forcing you to recognize, help, or even heal one another.

When I said that entering the Kingdom of God is the great adventure the Lord offers us every day by discovering His plan for us, and not just ours for Him—I call it 'Connecting the Dots.' Do you remember that coloring book where we didn't see the whole picture until we looked for and found the next dot to connect them all? For me, this has been and continues to be the most exciting way discover and do God's Will.

This is how it works for me. I have my list of things I want or have to do each day, but I am open and look for God's dots that start connecting.

Then the more I connect them, the more I know it's not a coincidence, but Him revealing His Will to me for the person or the situation I'm in. The moment I 'get it' and see the whole picture, I can sense the Lord with me, offering His answer to a prayer. Many times, He answers mine at the same time through a person or the situation I'm in. When it's over, there is the realization that this was a moment and experience, because we connected the dots.

STORYTIME:

The windshield on my car was hit by a stone and cracked. Besides being another thing I had to do, the only time they could get me in to fix it was a day that I was booked and busy. Pain in the neck I thought. So, I started the day frustrated and overwhelmed because of having to rush across town get the darn windshield fixed so I could get on with what I had to do. After I checked in I was told that it would take an hour and a half. Great news! So, there I sat in the waiting room mumbling to myself and to the Lord, "Why me?" Sound familiar?

The minute I sat down, a young woman came in to have her windshield fixed. When she sat down, I sensed that she was troubled. After the usual hello and casual talk, I asked her if she was ok. She began to cry and told me that she had just come from the hospital where she said her mother was dying, but had come to get her windshield fixed because it was the only time they could fit her in.

We began to talk at length and I shared with her what the Lord had taught me about suffering and death, and how He is with us to help us through it. At the end I asked her if I could pray with her to experience the Lord with her and her mother. She said "Yes" and welcomed it. So we prayed, and all during the prayer she wept and let out all the fear and worrying that she held inside.

After we prayed, she gave me a hug and said "I think the Lord sent you." **Bingo**! We 'connected the dots'. Both of us thought that the reason we had the same appointment time was to get our windows fixed. That was our plan, but the Lord's plan was that each of us was the answer to each other's prayer. I immediately realized that this was the Lord's plan all along for me. That's why my response to her saying that God had sent me was, "He did."

Connecting the dots is the most exciting way that the Lord reveals His will every day. I strongly suggest you ask the Lord to reveal His will for you by giving you the gift of looking for and recognizing **'the non-coincidence dots'**.

The Locksmith

Oh, to be forgiven!

Truly forgiven!

Like the dawn of a new day

the Son rises within,

and a new horizon shines in every part of my being.

Wake up! Rise up!

And give thanks to God!

The Son is shining and has awoken within me a BRIGHT new day!

Oh, to forgive!

Chains of resentment are broken,

Bitter memories fade.

For as much as I forgive, I am forgiven, and the past no longer holds me in bound.

No longer under the slavery of their judgement,

No longer can I hold others in the chains of my own shortsightedness.
A new horizon spreads before me. The path is long and narrow, the Son shines brightly to light the way. His arms outstretched, He invites "come FOLLOW me."

Oh, to find acceptance,

within acceptance the chains of selfishness

and self-centeredness are loosed.

The veil that separated me from others is lifted, I see clearly now....

A brightness, a future, a light unfiltered.

Now able to see goodness in others,

God's Son shining again.

As we walk down the pathway of life I see others along the way, their arms outstretched, their faces veiled.

They, too, are bound to the world with chains of hopelessness and despair.

He has given me the keys to unlock their suffering, He has given me a desire to draw them near.

He has given us a light to stay on the path...

and the hands join ours.

The chain becomes human,

closely linked and firmly joined

to follow the master locksmith, Jesus.

Spiritual Director, Sally Kazin

NOTES

I have written a year-long devotional called **Strength for Your Journey**, and I added **Strength for Your Journey Devotional Companion** to go with it. Both are available in Spanish and have received the Imprimatur and Nihil Obstat.

Many have developed a deeper understanding of who they are in God's eyes, and they learned many helpful tools to aid them along their faith journeys through these guides. This led me to write this abbreviated version called **Invitation to Intimacy With God.**

My hope is that this edition will help those who are not yet inclined to take on a year-long study but still want to gain the habit of journaling and pondering in the effort of gaining a closer relationship to God. Take this as an opportunity to apply your faith among daily living.

This edition may also be used for group study purposes. It is an ideal tool for faith building, not only for individuals, but also for parish communities.

If you decide to use this as a group study, I recommend that you meet once a week at the same time, and do not exceed ten people in a group.

Here are some tips that will help you get the most out of your meetings and sharing.

I liken God to a diamond; there are many facets to a diamond. It is in the sacred moments of sharing and listening within the group that we are privileged to experience those many facets.

So while sharing:

- Do not hide behind words like "we", "us", or "people". You are only to share your own feeling, experience, or opinion.
- Do not invite or start a discussion. Do not solicit anything outside this program.
- Do not exhort or preach to yourself or others.
- Do not rush. Take your time, since good sharing is gradual and calls for pauses.
- Do not take notes during the sharing session.
- Maintain confidentiality. Please do not speak about what you have heard during the meeting or after the meeting to anyone.

While listening:

- Do not judge or condemn. Other's feelings are neither right nor wrong. Try to feel their feelings.
- Do not probe; do not interrogate.
- Do not fix it; do not give advice.
- Do not ask questions.
- Do not interrupt the silence. Give time to pause while a team member is sharing.

CONCORDANCE

FAITH

Faith…green… Just as the green earth is the foundation for the physical building; Faith is the foundation for the building of our spiritual life.

1. Faith is the realization of what is hoped for and evidence of things not seen. **Hebrews 11:1**
2. For whatever is born of God overcomes the world; and this is the victory that has overcome the world—our faith. **1 John 5:4**
3. And though you have not seen Him, you love Him, and though you do not see Him now, but believe in Him, you greatly rejoice with joy inexpressible and full of glory, obtaining as the outcome of your faith the salvation of your souls. **1 Peter 1:8-9**
4. But the Spirit explicitly says that in later times some will fall away from the faith, paying attention to deceitful spirits and doctrines of demons. **1 Timothy 4:1**
5. Fight the good fight of faith; take hold of the eternal life to which you were called, and you made the good confession in the presence of many witnesses. **1 Timothy 6:12**
6. For we live by faith, not by sight. **2 Corinthians 5:7**
7. To this end also we pray for you always, that our God will count you worthy of your calling and fulfill every desire for goodness and the work of faith with power. **2 Thessalonians 1:11**
8. I have fought the good fight, I have finished the course, I have kept the faith. **2 Timothy 4:7**

9. I will deliver you from the Jewish people, as well as from the Gentiles, to whom I now send you, to open their eyes, in order to turn them from darkness to light, and from the power of Satan to God, that they may receive forgiveness of sins and an inheritance among those who are sanctified by faith in Me. **Acts 26:17-18**

10. For it is by grace you have been saved, through faith— and this is not from yourselves, it is the gift of God. **Ephesians 2:8**

11. There is one body and one Spirit, just as you were called to one hope when you were called; one Lord, one faith, one baptism; one God and Father of all, who is over all and through all and in all. **Ephesians 4:4-6**

12. In addition to all this, take up the shield of faith, with which you can extinguish all the flaming arrows of the evil one. **Ephesians 6:16**

13. Know that a person is not justified by the works of the law, but by faith in Jesus Christ. So, we, too, have put our faith in Christ Jesus that we may be justified by faith in Christ and not by the works of the law, because by theworks of the law no one will be justified. **Galatians 2:16**

14. I have been crucified with Christ and I no longer live, but Christ lives in me. The life I now live in the body, I live by faith in the Son of God, who loved me and gave himself for me. **Galatians 2:20**

15. I would like to learn just one thing from you: Did you receive the Spirit by the works of the law, or by hearing of faith? **Galatians 3:2**

16. For you are all sons of God through faith in Christ Jesus. For all of you who were baptized into Christ have clothed yourselves with Christ. **Galatians 3:26-27**

17. For in Christ Jesus neither circumcision nor uncircumcision has any value. The only thing that counts is faith expressing itself through love. **Galatians 5:6**

18. Let us draw near to God with a sincere heart and with the full assurance that faith brings, having our hearts sprinkled to cleanse us from a guilty conscience and having our bodies washed with pure water. **Hebrews 10:22**

19. But my righteous one will live by faith. And I take no pleasure in the one who shrinks back. **Hebrews 10:38**

20. Now faith is confidence in what we hope for and assurance about what we do not see. **Hebrews 11:1**

21. And without faith it is impossible to please God because anyone who comes to him must believe that he exists and that he rewards those who earnestly seek him. **Hebrews 11:6**

22. You know that the testing of your faith produces perseverance. **James 1:3**

23. In the same way, faith by itself, if it is not accompanied by action, is dead. **James 2:17**

24. And the prayer offered in faith will make the sick person well; the Lord will raise them up. If they have sinned, they will be forgiven. Therefore, confess your sins to each other and pray for each other so that you may be healed. The prayer of a righteous person is powerful and effective. **James 5:15-16**

25. But you, dear friends, build yourselves up in your most holy faith, praying in the Holy Spirit. **Jude 1:20**

26. Jesus said to them, "Because you have so little faith— Truly I tell you, if you have faith as small as a mustard seed, you can say to this mountain, 'Move from here to there,' and it will move. Nothing will be impossible for you." **Matthew 17:20**

27. Jesus turned and saw her. "Take heart, daughter," he said, "your faith has healed you." And the woman was healed at that moment. **Matthew 9:22**

28. For in the gospel the righteousness of God is revealed—a righteousness that is by faith from first to last, just as it is written: "The righteous will live by faith." **Romans 1:17**

29. Consequently, faith comes from hearing the message, and the message is heard through the word about Christ. **Romans 10:17**

30. For we maintain that a person is justified by faith apart from the works of the law. **Romans 3:28**

31. However, to the one who does not work but trusts God who justifies the ungodly, their faith is credited as righteousness. **Romans 4:5**

32. Through whom we have gained access by faith into this grace in which we now stand. And we boast in the hope of the glory of God. **Romans 5:2**

Notes

TRUST

Trust...diamond...The perfect diamond is truly crystal clear, harder than steel and flawless. One who trusts in the Lord sees through their daily trials as if they were transparent. It is through those trials that one can see the Lord's abiding love. They see that trust in Him is perfect...flawless, thereby, they are not easily broken.

1. While being reviled, He did not revile in return; while suffering, He uttered no threats, but kept entrusting Himself to Him who judges righteously. **1 Peter 2:23**
2. Trust in the Lord forever, for in God the Lord, we have an everlasting Rock. **Isaiah 26:4**
3. Who is among you that fears the Lord, that obeys the voice of His servant, that walks in darkness and has no light? Let him trust in the name of the Lord and rely on his God. **Isaiah 50:10**
4. Blessed is the one who trusts in the Lord, and whose trust is the Lord. **Jeremiah 17:7**
5. Those who trust in their riches will fall, but the righteous will thrive like a green leaf. **Proverbs 11:2)**
6. He who gives attention to the word will find good, and blessed is he who trusts in the Lord. **Proverbs 16:20**
7. So that your trust may be in the Lord, I teach you today, even you. **Proverbs 22:19**
8. Trust in the Lord with all your heart and do not lean on your own understanding. **Proverbs 3:5**
9. It is better to take refuge in the Lord than to trust in man. **Psalm 118:8**
10. So I will have an answer for him who reproaches me, for I trust in your word. **Psalm 119:42**

11. Let me hear your loving kindness in the morning for I trust in you; teach me the way in which I should walk; for to you I lift up my soul. **Psalm 143:8**

12. In you our fathers trusted; they trusted and you delivered them. To you they cried out and were delivered; in you they trusted and were not disappointed. **Psalm 22:45**

13. The Lord is my strength and my shield; my heart trusts in him, and he helps me. My heart leaps for joy, and with my song I shall thank him. **Psalm 28:7**

14. But I trust in you, Lord; I say, "You are my God." **Psalm 31:14**

15. Many are the woes of the wicked, but the Lord's unfailing love surrounds the one who trusts in him. **Psalm 32:10**

16. Our soul waits for the Lord; He is our help and our shield. for our heart rejoices in Him, because we trust in His holy name. **Psalm 33:20-21**

17. O taste and see that the Lord is good; blessed is the one who trusts and takes refuge in him. **Psalm 34:8**

18. Trust in the Lord and do good; dwell in the land and cultivate faithfulness. **Psalm 37:3**

19. Commit your way to the Lord; trust also in him and he will do it. **Psalm 37:5**

20. Offer the sacrifices of the righteous and trust in the Lord. (**Psalm 4:5**)

21. In God, whose word I praise, in God I trust and am not afraid. What can mere mortals do to me? **Psalm 56:4**

22. They were helped against them, and the Hagrites and all who were with them were given into their hand; for they cried out to God in the battle, and He answered their prayers because they trusted in Him. **1 Chronicles 5:20**

23. And those who know your name put their trust in you, for you, O LORD, have not forsaken those who seek you. **Psalm 9:10**

24. In you our fathers trusted; they trusted, and you delivered them. To you they cried, and were saved; in you they trusted, and were not disappointed. **Psalm 22:4-5**

25. Behold, God is my salvation; I will trust, and will not be afraid; for the LORD GOD is my strength and my song, and he has become my salvation. **Isaiah 12:2**

26. Then the king was very pleased and gave orders for Daniel to be taken up out of the den. So Daniel was taken up out of the den and no injury whatever was found on him, because he had trusted in his God. **Daniel 6:23**

27. Thus says the Lord, "Cursed is the man who trusts in mankind and makes flesh his strength, and whose heart turns away from the Lord. **Jeramiah 17:5**

28. For because of your trust in your own achievement and treasures, even you yourself will be captured; and Chemosh will go off into exile together with his priests and his princes. **Jeremiah 48:7**

29. For our heart rejoices in Him, because we trust in His holy name. **Psalm 33:21**

30. For I will not trust in my bow, nor will my sword save me. But You have saved us from our adversaries, and You have put to shame those who hate us. **Psalm 44:6-7**

LOVE

Love…red…the heart is the center of the body bringing forth life, giving nutrients to all other parts of the body. Without it, the body cannot function. So also, love is the heart of our spiritual body…the body of Christ. Love calls us to forget ourselves and to give freely by using all the gifts that we have been given. Thus, the body of Christ becomes a life-giving organism throughout the world.

1. And He said to him, "'You shall love the Lord your God with all your heart, and with all your soul, and with all your mind.' This is the great and foremost commandment. **Matthew 22:37-38**
2. You shall love your neighbor as yourself. There is no other commandment greater than these. **Mark 12:31**
3. Right, Teacher; You have truly stated that He is One, and there is no one else besides Him; and to love Him with all the heart and with all the understanding and with all the strength, and to love one's neighbor as himself, is much more than all burnt offerings and sacrifices. **Mark 12:32-33**
4. By this, love is perfected with us, so that we may have confidence in the day of judgment; because as He is, so also are we in this world. **1 John 4:17**
5. There is no fear in love; but perfect love casts out fear, because fear involves punishment, and the one who fears is not perfected in love. **1 John 4:18**
6. We love, because He first loved us. **1 John 4:19**
7. A new commandment I give to you, that you love one another, even as I have loved you, that you also love one another. **John 13:34**
8. If I speak with the tongues of men and of angels, but do not have love, I have become a noisy gong or a clanging cymbal. **1 Corinthians 13:1**

9. If I have the gift of prophecy and know all mysteries and all knowledge; and if I have all faith so as to remove mountains, but do not have love, I am nothing. **1 Corinthians 13:2**

10. And if I give all my possessions to feed the poor, and if I surrender my body to be burned, but do not have love, it profits me nothing. **1 Corinthians 13:3**

11. Love is patient, love is kind and is not jealous; love does not brag and is not arrogant, does not act unbecomingly; it does not seek its own, is not provoked, does not take into account a wrong suffered, does not rejoice in unrighteousness, but rejoices with the truth. **1 Corinthians 13:4-6**

12. Love bears all things, believes all things, hopes all things, endures all things. **1 Corinthians 13:7**

13. Love never fails; but if there are gifts of prophecy, they will be done away; if there are tongues, they will cease; if there is knowledge, it will be done away. **1 Corinthians 13:8**

14. But now faith, hope, love, abide these three; but the greatest of these is love. **1 Corinthians 13:13**

15. I have been crucified with Christ; and it is no longer I who live, but Christ lives in me; and the life which I now live in the flesh I live by faith in the Son of God, who loved me and gave Himself up for me. **Galatians 2:20**

16. Husbands, love your wives, just as Christ also loved the church and gave Himself up for her. **Ephesians 5:25**

17. That Christ may dwell in your hearts through faith; and that you, being rooted and grounded in love, may be able to comprehend with all the [a]saints what is the breadthand length and height and depth, 19 and to know the love of Christ which surpasses knowledge, that you may be filled up to all the fullness of God. **Ephesians 3:17-19**

18. Now may our Lord Jesus Christ Himself and God our Father, who has loved us and given us eternal comfort and good hope by grace. **2 Thessalonians 2:16**

19. But when the kindness of God our Savior and His love for mankind appeared, He saved us, not on the basis of deeds which we have done in righteousness, but according to His mercy, by the washing of regeneration and renewing by the Holy Spirit. **Titus 3:4-5**

20. Each one must do just as he has purposed in his heart, not grudgingly or under compulsion, for God loves a cheerful giver.
2 Corinthians 9:7

21. Each one must do just as he has purposed in his heart, not grudgingly or under compulsion, for God loves a cheerful giver.
2 Corinthians 9:7

22. But God, being rich in mercy, because of His great love with which He loved us, even when we were dead in our transgressions, made us alive together with Christ. **Ephesians 2:4-5**

23. Beloved, let us love one another, for love is from God; and everyone who loves is born of God and knows God. **1 John 4:7**

24. The one who does not love does not know God, for God is love. By this the love of God was manifested in us that God has sent His only begotten Son into the world so that we might live through Him. In this is love, not that we loved God, but that He loved us and sent His Son to be the propitiation for our sins. **1 John 4:8-10**

25. Beloved, if God so loved us, we also ought to love one another. No one has seen God at any time; if we love one another, God abides in us, and His love is perfected in us. **1 John 4:11-12**

26. May the Lord direct your hearts into the love of God and into the steadfastness of Christ. **2 Thessalonians 3:5**

27. Do not love the world nor the things in the world. If anyone loves the world, the love of the Father is not in him. For all that is in the world, the lust of the flesh and the lust of the eyes and the boastful pride of life, is not from the Father, but is from the world. The world is passing away, and also its lusts; but the one who does the will of God lives forever. **1 John 2:15-17**

28. But whoever keeps His word, in him the love of God has truly been perfected. By this we know that we are in Him. **1 John 2:5**
29. See how great a love the Father has bestowed on us, that we would be called children of God; and such we are. For this reason, the world does not know us, because it did not know Him. Beloved, now we are children of God, and it has not appeared yet what we will be. We know that when He appears, we will be like Him, because we will see Him just as He is. **1 John 3:1-2**
30. But in all these things we overwhelmingly conquer through Him who loved us. **Romans 8:37**

Notes

OBEDIENCE

Obedience…deep blue…The color of the ocean…without water all life withers and dies. Without obedience, our spiritual life withers and dies. We must be willing to submit our will to the Lord and say, "Your will be done" if we wish to feed our spiritual life and keep it alive. Obedience is oddly enough, a key to freedom.

1. The one who says, "I have come to know Him," and does not keep (obey) His commandments, is a liar, and the truth is not in him. **1 John 2:4**

2. Whatever we ask we receive from Him, because we keep/ obey His commandments and do the things that are pleasing in His sight. **1 John 3:22**

3. As obedient children, do not be conformed to the former lusts which were yours in your ignorance, but like the Holy One who called you, be holy yourselves also in all your behavior. **1 Peter 1:14-15**

4. Since you have in obedience to the truth purified your souls for a sincere love of the brethren, fervently love one another from the heart, for you have been born again not of seed which is perishable but imperishable, that is, through the living and enduring word of God. **1 Peter 1:22-23**

5. Because of the proof given by this ministry, they will glorify God for your obedience to your confession of the gospel of Christ and for the liberality of your contribution to them and to all. **2 Corinthians 9:13**

6. Peter & the apostles answered, "We must obey God rather than men" **Acts 5:29**

7. Slaves, in all things obey those who are your masters on earth, not with external service, as those who merely please men, but with sincerity of heart, fearing the Lord. **Colossians 3:22**

8. See, I am setting before you today a blessing and a curse: the blessing, if you listen to the commandments of the Lord your God, which I am commanding you today; and the curse, if you do not listen to the commandments of the Lord your God, but turn aside from the way which I am commanding you today, by following other gods which you have not known. **Deuteronomy 11:26-28**

9. Be careful to listen to all these words which I command you, so that it may be well with you and your sons after you forever, for you will be doing what is good and right in the sight of the Lord your God. **Deuteronomy 12:28**

10. Children, obey your parents in the Lord, for this is right. **Ephesians 6:1**

11. You were running well; who hindered you from obeying the truth? **Galatians 5:7**

12. You shall follow the Lord your God and fear Him; and you shall keep His commandments, listen to His voice, serve Him, and cling to Him. **Deuteronomy 13:4**

13. Obey your leaders and submit to them, for they keep watch over your souls as those who will give an account. Let them do this with joy and not with grief, for this would be unprofitable for you. **Hebrews 13:17**

14. Although He was a Son, He learned obedience from the things which He suffered, and having been made perfect, He became to all those who obey Him the source of eternal salvation. **Hebrews 5:8-9**

15. But to the Lord, our God, belong compassion and forgiveness, though we rebelled against. **Daniel 9:9**

16. But one who looks intently at the perfect law, the law of liberty, and abides by it, not having become a forgetful hearer but an effectual doer, this man will be blessed in what he does. **James 1:25**

17. John the Baptist appeared in the desert proclaiming a baptism of repentance for the forgiveness of sins. **Mark 1:4**

18. If you love Me, you will keep My commandments. **John 14:15**

19. If you keep My commandments, you will abide in My love; just as I have kept My Father's commandments and abide in His love. **John 15:10**

20. But He said, "On the contrary, blessed are those who hear the word of God and observe it." **Luke 11:28**

21. Being found in appearance as a man, He humbled Himself by becoming obedient to the point of death, even death on a cross. **Philippians 2:8**

22. The wise of heart will receive commands, but a babbling fool will be ruined. **Proverbs 10:8**

23. I considered my ways and turned my feet to obey Your testimonies. **Psalm 119:59**

24. Because of the greatness of Your power Your enemies will give feigned obedience to You. **Psalm 66:3**

25. Jesus Christ our Lord, through whom we have received grace and apostleship to bring about the obedience of faith among all the Gentiles for His name's sake. **Romans 1:5**

26. For as through the one man's disobedience the many were made sinners, even so through the obedience of the One the many will be made righteous. **Romans 5:19**

27. Do you not know that when you present yourselves to someone as slaves for obedience, you are slaves of the one whom you obey, either of sin resulting in death, or of obedience resulting in righteousness? **Romans 6:16**

28. For the report of your obedience has reached to all; therefore, I am rejoicing over you, but I want you to be wise in what is good and innocent in what is evil. **Romans 16:19**

29. His affection abounds all the more toward you, as he remembers the obedience of you all, how you received him with fear and trembling. **2 Corinthians 7:15**

BIBLIOGRAPHY

1. Keys To Freedom, Faith, Trust, Love, Obedience. Linda Rose, co. 1999
2. Boot Camp For The Kingdom Of Heaven, Linda Rose, co. 2010
3. Descripton of Faith Key, Linda Rose and Bob Dudley, co. 2000
4. Description of Trust Key, Linda Rose and Bob Dudley, co. 2000
5. "Letter From God" www.fathersloveletter.com copyrighted
6. Description of Love Key, Linda Rose and Bob Dudley, co. 2000
7. Description of Obedience Key, Linda Rose and Bob Dudley, co. 2000

Scripture references include:

New International Version, revised Edition

New International Version Biblegateway.com, Bible.USCCB.org

Made in the USA
Columbia, SC
29 January 2025